Editor
Polly Hoffman

Editorial Project Manager
Mara Ellen Guckian

Editor-in-Chief
Sharon Coan, M.S. Ed.

Illustrators
Kevin Barnes
Renée Christine Yates

Cover Artist
Barb Lorseyedi

Art Coordinator
Kevin Barnes

Art Director
Cjae Froshay

Imaging
Ralph Olmedo, Jr.
James Edward Grace

Product Manager
Phil Garcia

Publisher
Mary D. Smith, M.S. Ed.

Full Color
Literacy Centers for
Reading Skills

K-2

Authors

Dede Dodds, M.S. Ed. & Traci Clausen, M.S. Ed

Teacher Created Resources, Inc.
6421 Industry Way
Westminster, CA 92683
www.teachercreated.com

ISBN-0-7439-3703-1

©2003 Teacher Created Resources, Inc

Reprinted, 2005

Made in U.S.A.

Table of Contents

Introduction

Purposeful practice is essential for improvement and mastery of literacy skills. All students can experience literacy success, given proper instruction, materials, and plenty of opportunities to practice. Primary teachers will find *Literacy Centers for Reading Skills (K–2)* invaluable in providing this much-needed practice. The centers should be used to review and reinforce the language skills and objectives taught as part of your reading, writing, listening, and speaking curriculum.

This book includes meaningful, easy-to-create, easy-to-manage, independent activities for primary classrooms. These literacy centers supply the independent practice that is a natural follow-up to whole class instruction. Teacher-directed lessons are most effective if the materials and activities involved are available to small groups or individuals for further investigation. Students need to practice what they have learned in order to assimilate the new information into their current knowledge base. Through centers, students gain opportunities to manipulate, repeat, share, and expand upon the presented materials at their own pace.

Grade level and/or ability level adjustments should be made as teachers and aides create the literacy centers. Center directions inform teachers of all the necessary materials and preparation. Centers should be created to accomodate standards and to incorporate current classroom texts, sight word lists, etc.

Keep in mind that children learn best when they are actively involved in their own learning process. Classrooms incorporating literacy centers into their daily routine become less teacher directed and more student driven. As students' knowledge grows, they learn to think critically, make decisions, and solve problems. They also demonstrate the personal characteristics of responsibility, self-esteem, self-management, and integrity needed to function in society.

What You Will Find in This Book

There are several literacy center activities for each component. Each literacy center begins with an objective. The teacher's instructions are presented in several steps. These instructions allow the teacher to present the activity as a directed, group activity prior to placing it in a center. Often, scripted text will appear in italics to aid the teacher in presenting a lesson.

Each teacher page includes details about what you will need, how to create the manipulatives for the center, how to present the center, tips for teaching it, things to keep in mind, extension ideas, and home connection suggestions.

There is a student task card for each literacy center with simple instructions designed to remind the student what to do during the activity. Recording sheets and patterns are included when appropriate.

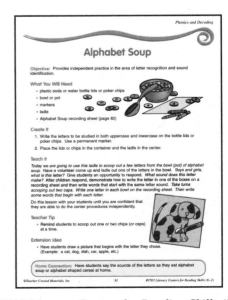

What is a Literacy Center?

A *literacy center* is an effective teaching tool developed to support (follow up) and reinforce whole group instruction. Literacy centers offer teachers a way to engage students of various abilities in active learning. Literacy centers allow students to work independently, thus freeing up the teacher to focus on differentiated instruction. Centers are designed to provide inviting activities where one or more students can work independently at a given time. Various learning tasks, along with various degrees of teacher interaction, are involved.

Centers provide learning motivation by making practice fun and non-threatening. The literacy centers in this book are process-oriented. The centers offer opportunities for students to practice new skills and to problem solve at their own pace.

Once the standards, skills, and objectives have been taught formally, students need time to practice with the materials in order to set each skill (objective) and master it.

Why Are Literacy Centers Valuable?

An optimal learning environment is created when whole-group, teacher-directed, instructional periods are combined with reinforcement and independent practice in student literacy centers. Too often in the educational process, the emphasis is placed on teaching, rather than on learning. A literacy center places the emphasis on the individual needs of each student. Research affirms the value of literacy centers and emphasizes several instructional advantages:

- Literacy centers address different learning styles better than paper and pencil tasks; they also motivate students more by providing varied stimulating activities. (Wait & Stephens, 1989)

- Literacy centers result in improved communication between home and school. (Optiz, 1995)

- Literacy centers play an important role in meeting the needs of each child. (Huyett, 1994)

Literacy centers (managed in small groups) create cooperative learning relationships. Learning language is a social activity. In most situations, centers allow classmates (no matter what the level) opportunities to bounce ideas off each other and to practice new skills.

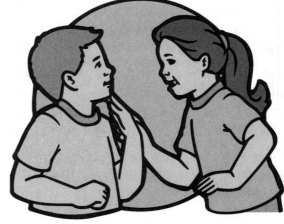

There is no better way for students to truly learn a skill or concept than to work together to communicate among classmates and teach others what they have mastered.

The Language Arts Components

The three language arts components included in *Literacy Centers for Reading Skills (K–2)* are Sight Words, Phonics and Decoding, and Reading and Writing Responses to Literature.

Sight Words

The Sight Words component deals with the first three hundred most commonly used sight words from Dr. Fry's Instant Sight Words. These sight words have been scientifically determined to be the most commonly used words in the English language. This list is a basic tool for reading and writing teachers, curriculum developers, literacy tutors, authors of children's books, and researchers.

Sight words are words that appear over-and-over again in written text. These words must be internalized, or memorized, so that each of these high frequency words can be read by sight and does not need to be sounded out. The ability to read these words instantly greatly increases reading fluency and comprehension.

The activities found in the Sight Words component will expedite retention of these important words. Another reason for learning these words is that many of the frequently-used words do not follow regular phonics rules. For example, how do you sound out *of* or *said*? The answer is that beginning readers need to learn to read these words by "sight." Beginning writers also need to learn to spell these common words.

Phonics and Decoding

Phonics and decoding skills are practiced in any lesson or activity that includes print. Whenever a student is hearing sounds while attending to print, phonics instruction and practice are occurring. "Phonics and decoding" refers to the association of letters (graphemes) and the sounds (phonemes) they represent. The application of these phonics skills to reading and to writing is referred to as "decoding and encoding."

A key strategy in this component is to group words with similar patterns or rimes (phonograms). In word families like cat, sat, flat, or king, ring, wing, each word contains the same pattern or "chunk". Once the pattern is internalized, readers can generalize to other words with similar rimes. This component includes most frequently used chunks or rimes as identified by researchers (Wylie & Durrell, 1970; Fry, 1998).

Reading and Writing Response

Responding to different forms of literature enables students to voice their own opinions, demonstrate their comprehension of the text, and share their interpretations of the story. A natural way for students to explore the phonics of language is to respond in writing to what they have heard or read. Frequent writing does more to increase spelling achievement than any other single activity. Writing helps the student discover the function of alphabetic spelling and the way words are formed.

What is the Teacher's Role?

Teachers implementing *Literacy Centers for Reading Skills (K–2)* in their classrooms should do the following as part of their preparation and presentation of a center:

- Choose appropriate center activities for the ability and developmental levels of students.

- Select literacy centers based on specific curriculum standards.

- Teach skills, objectives, and concepts formally through whole-group lessons prior to implementing independent activities.

- Create and set up fun, attractive, and motivating centers.

- Establish a classroom management plan clearly defining expectations.

- Explain procedures and demonstrate particular behaviors for each center.

- Afford many opportunities to interact with and practice previously taught skills at the centers.

- Create a non-threatening, supportive learning environment for all students.

- Monitor student progress toward mastery by assessing student performances and/or student recording sheets.

- Give meaningful feedback, re-teaching and adjusting when necessary.

- Offer extensions and challenges when appropriate.

Standards and Assessments

In this section you will find a grid detailing the literacy standards practiced using the activities suggested. *Literacy Centers for Reading Skills (K–2)* was designed with the K–2 teacher in mind. Therefore, the standards met by the book go across these grade levels and fit well within broad literacy standards.

Teachers will find information within this section on both formal and informal assessment with respect to the use of literacy centers. The main objective for centers is to facilitate small group teaching and practice among students.

Formal assessment is not an emphasis of this book. Due to the nature of centers, student assessment is not always concrete or authentic. However, there are different ways to assess student progress toward mastery. Students demonstrate their development of concept knowledge in a variety of ways. Listed below are assessment alternatives that keep the students accountable for their learning.

❁ Recording Answers

Provide students with recording sheets. Instructions for each recording sheet will vary based on the activities and concepts being practiced. The sheets should be collected and reviewed. A response, although not always necessary, can be given in the form of a sticker, a note, or a grade.

❁ Checking Each Other

When working cooperatively, young learners naturally monitor each other and provide support. Encourage them to work with and check each other. If a student feels that another student may have the wrong answer, the student performing the activity may try again. In doing this, all of the students are engaged and encouraged.

❁ Getting an "Expert"

Identify a child who has mastered the center. Assign him or her the job of being that center's "expert." Instruct students to ask the "expert" to come to the center (even if it is necessary to interrupt him or her and check their work. Often the mini-lesson given by that classmate is a more effective one than that of the paid expert (the classroom teacher). Teach the "expert" to "instruct" with words, not hands.

❁ Using an Answer Key

Answer keys for center activities can be placed in various places for student use. Below are some options for answer key usage:

- Set aside a place in the classroom (teacher's desk, counter, extra desk, etc.) where answer keys can be found.
- Provide an answer key with the center materials.
- Assign a student the position of "answer key monitor". That student will pass out answer keys to those students who have completed the task assigned.

Standards and Benchmarks

1 Demonstrates competence in the general skills and strategies of the writing process

1a Uses prewriting strategies to plan written work
Categories
Retell the Story

1b Uses strategies to draft and revise written work
Categories
Use the Clues

1c Uses strategies to edit and publish written work
Ask the Author

1d Evaluates own and others' writing
Ask the Author
Blooming Questions
Convince Me

1e Dictates or writes with a logical sequence
Retell the Story

1f Dictates or writes detailed descriptions of familiar persons, places, objects, or experiences
Labels, Labels, Labels
Retell the Story

1g Writes in response to literature
Ask the Author
Blooming Questions
Retell the Story
Convince Me

1h Writes in a variety of formats
Ask the Author
Retell the Story

2 Demonstrates competence in the stylistic and rhetorical aspects of writing

2a Uses general, frequently used words to convey basic ideas
Retell the Story
Would You Rather?

Standards and Benchmarks *(cont.)*

3 Uses grammatical and mechanical conventions in written compositions

3a *Forms letters in print and spaces words and sentences*

Capture the Consonants

Fishing for Sight Words

Pick-a-Word

Retell the Story

Convince Me

Name Game

Making Little Words

Use the Clues

Would You Rather?

3b *Uses complete sentences*

Name Game

Use the Clues

Retell the Story

Convince Me

Fishing for Sight Words

Blooming Questions

Would You Rather?

3c *Uses declarative and interrogative sentences in written compositions*

Use the Clues

Blooming Questions

Retell the Story

Would You Rather?

3d *Uses nouns in written compositions*

Categories

3e *Uses verbs in written compositions*

Use the Clues

3f *Uses adjectives in written compositions (e.g., uses descriptive words)*

Use the Clues

3g *Uses adverbs in written compositions (i.e., uses words that answer how, when, where, and why questions)*

Ask the Author

3h *Uses conventions of spelling in written compositions (e.g., spells high frequency, commonly misspelled words from appropriate grade-level list; uses a dictionary and other resources to spell words; spells own first and last name)*

Newspaper Search

Would You Rather?

Blooming Questions

Name Game

Use the Clues

Retell the Story

Standards and Benchmarks *(cont.)*

3i *Uses conventions of capitalization in written compositions (e.g., first and last names, first word of a sentence)*

    Name Game

    Use the Clues

    Retell the Story

    Convince Me

3j *Uses conventions of punctuation in written compositions (e.g., uses periods after declarative sentences, uses question marks after interrogative sentences, uses commas in a series of words)*

    Name Game

    Labels, Labels, Labels

    Ask the Author

    Retell the Story

    Would You Rather?

    Convince Me

4 Gathers and uses information for research purposes

4a *Uses a variety of strategies to identify topics to investigate*

    Categories

    Ask the Author

    Blooming Questions

    Convince Me

4b *Generates questions about topics of personal interest*

    Categories

    Ask the Author

    Would You Rather?

    Convince Me

4c *Uses books to gather information for research topics*

    Book Talk

Standards and Benchmarks *(cont.)*

5 Demonstrates competence in the skills and strategies of the reading process

    5a Understands that print conveys meaning
- Pick-a-Word
- Retell the Story

    5b Understands how print is organized and read
- Pick-a-Word
- Use the Clues
- Blooming Questions
- Retell the Story

    5c Creates mental images from pictures and print
- Concentration
- Making Little Words
- Newspaper Search
- Labels, Labels, Labels

    5d Uses picture clues and captions to aid comprehension and to make predictions about content
- Partner Reading
- Blooming Questions

    5e Decodes unknown words using basic elements of phonics analysis and structural analysis
- Capture the Consonants
- Name Game
- Concentration
- Fishing for Sight Words
- Making Little Words
- Newspaper Search
- Categories
- Partner Reading
- Pick-a-Word
- Use the Clues
- Retell the Story

Standards and Benchmarks *(cont.)*

5f *Uses Picture Dictionary to determine word meanings*
   Categories
5g *Uses self-correction strategies*
   Partner Reading
5h *Reads familiar stories, poems, and passages aloud*
   Partner Reading

6 Demonstrates competence in the general skills and strategies for reading a variety of literary texts

6a *Applies reading skills and strategies to a variety of familiar literary passages and texts (e.g., fairy tales, folk tales, fiction, nonfiction, legends, fables, myths, poems, picture books, predictable books)*
   Partner Reading
   Retell the Story

6b *Identifies favorite books and stories*
   Partner Reading
   Ask the Author
   Blooming Questions

6c *Identifies setting, main characters, main events, and problems in stories*
   Retell the Story

6d *Makes simple inferences regarding the order of events and possible outcomes*
   Partner Reading
   Ask the Author
   Blooming Questions

6e *Identifies the main ideas or theme of a story*
   Partner Reading
   Retell the Story

6f *Relates stories to personal experiences*
   Partner Reading
   Ask the Author
   Blooming Questions

Standards and Benchmarks *(cont.)*

7 **Demonstrates competence in the general skills and strategies for reading a variety of informational texts**

7a Applies reading skills and strategies to a variety of informational books

Newspaper Search   Categories

Partner Reading

7b Understands the main idea of simple expository information

Retell the Story

7c Summarizes information found in texts in his or her own words

Retell the Story

7d Relates new information to prior knowledge and experience

Ask the Author

Would You Rather?

8 **Demonstrates competence in speaking and listening as tools for learning**

8a Recognizes the characteristic sounds and rhythms of language

Pick-a-Word

8b Makes contributions in class and group discussions

Labels, Labels, Labels

Ask the Author

8c Asks and responds to questions

Use the Clues

Blooming Questions

8d Follows the rules of conversation (taking turns, staying on topic, raising hand to speak, etc.)

Concentration

Ask the Author

8e Uses different voice level, phrasing, and intonation for different situations

Partner Reading

8f Listens and responds to oral directions

All Center Activities

8g Listens and recites familiar stories, poems, and rhymes with patterns

Partner Reading

Book Talk

8h Listens and responds to a variety of media

Blooming Questions

Parent Support

Teaching is a partnership between teacher and child, teacher and parent, and parent and child. Parental support is an important component to effective teaching.

Each activity card lists Home Connection ideas to help the child bring the learning home. Use the letter on page 15 to advise parents of the Home Connection ideas. Simply write the suggestions in the box provided. Children can reinforce the concepts they have learned when they share homework with parents. By explaining what they are doing to others, they solidify their understanding of the skills and gain self-esteem in the process.

Technology Connections

If you have a computer available for student use, this is an excellent resource for extending and reinforcing literacy skills in the young learner. There are many interactive books currently available on CD that allow the child to hear a story read fluently and with meaningful expression. This activity builds phonemic awareness and vocabulary development as the child begins to associate the spoken word with the text on screen. Most interactive storybooks allow the child to click the mouse on a word they are unsure of, and hear it spoken aloud.

Even very young children can benefit from the use of a simple word processing or paint program (such as *Kid Pix*) to develop early writing skills. Simple activities that can reinforce basic literacy skills include: identifying letters of the alphabet on the keyboard; typing the beginning (or ending) letter of a word and drawing a picture or to represent that word; typing a simple rebus story; or even emailing a short note to grandma! These are all great exercises to help students realize the power of the written word. A print out of any of these activities to share with others is a great source of pride as well.

Home Connection Letter

Send the following letter home with each Home Connection activity.

Date:

Dear Parents,

Your child has been busy at school learning language skills through various reading, writing, listening, and speaking activities. Purposeful practice is essential in order for your child to master these skills and be a successful reader and writer.

Please help review and reinforce our classwork by doing the following activity together with your child:

Since many experts agree that parent involvement, no matter how great or small, helps children succeed at school, we thank you for your time and effort with this valuable practice.

Sincerely,

Management

Effective center activities rely greatly on successful management. This section offers many center management suggestions. Tips on using the cards, preparing the manipulatives, and the "center" process are included here. It is important to note that teachers must operate their centers in a way that best suits their style, classroom, and students. There is no one right way to organize and integrate centers within the classroom curriculum. Often, finding what works best is a process of trial and error.

Because students work at a variety of locations and on numerous activities with little teacher direction, the organization and management skills needed are numerous. Setting expectations, using positive reinforcement, and scheduling the day, are just the beginning when planning learning centers. There are many more tips that can help the teacher manage an effective literacy center classroom. Consider the following when implementing centers:

- Acceptable Noise Level
- Accountability Recording Sheets
- Changing Activities
- Classroom Rules
- Finish-up Time
- Grouping Students
- Introducing New Centers

- Limiting Center Numbers
- Literacy Center Folders
- Location and Rotation Chart
- Managing Materials
- Monitoring Choices
- Special Needs Students
- Using and Collecting Equipment

Some teachers wish to have just a few students at each area; some choose to have a center for each student. The primary factor in this decision should be the number of students you want working at each location. Some centers may vary in the number of students who can be accommodated for a given exercise. One way to plan is to divide the total number of students in the class by the number of students desired at each center. For example, in a class of twenty students, four literacy centers are needed if the teacher wishes to have five children at each center.

It is important to remember to provide center activities that your class is familiar with through formal instruction. Repetition of these activities is a useful learning tool for students and necessary when mastering skills. Repetition strengthens the basic lesson for some students, while offering improvisation and extension opportunities for others.

Literacy center time should be a fundamental part of the instructional day for each student. Center time should not simply be used as a reward for finishing a particular task or good behavior. All students should be allowed to participate in center activities.

Implementing Activity Cards

The primary concept behind *Literacy Centers for Reading Skills (K–2)* is that the centers provide independent practice. There are approximately six literacy center activities per category. Each activity is presented in several steps. First, present the activity as a directed whole-group activity or as a directed small-group activity. Then, present it as an official literacy center. Share the components, the process, and how to put the center away when finished.

Ease of use is at the core of a good center. The cards are simple and straightforward. Step-by-step instructions are provided describing how to prepare each center. The student cards can be laminated for durability. They provide simple, clear directions with illustrations. Ideally, the teacher will have instructed the students numerous times on how to perform the center activity. The student card will serve as a reminder for the student. The student card is not intended for use as instruction for a child who has not received prior instruction from a teacher. Each center must be taught (modeled) prior to its implementation in order to ensure future mastery of the skill being practiced. The teacher page consists of the following elements:

Objective
Each lesson has an objective for the area of practice.

What You Will Need
The materials required for the activity are listed here. Details are given on what needs to be purchased or made as far as manipulatives are concerned. Every effort has been made to provide as many finished, ready-to-use materials as possible in an effort to limit teacher prep time. Reproducible, blackline masters are provided. Many are open-ended to provide flexibility to best suit your curriculum and student ability levels. **Note:** When the term "any text" is listed in the materials list, teachers should provide students with appropriate reading material. Choose from an anthology story, a basal reader, a decodable book, or a weekly periodical such as *Time for Kids*.

Create It
The Create It section provides simple instructions on the few steps necessary to create each center activity.

Teach It
A directed lesson for each activity is included. Often, scripted words to present the lesson to the group are given in italics. The lesson is designed to teach the activity and is not intended as a lesson that teaches the literacy concept. Centers should reinforce previously taught concepts. Model the center activity for the students more than once. The activities should be chosen based on the literacy needs of your students and the curriculum areas you are currently teaching the students.

Literacy Center Folders

The utilization of literacy center folders in the implementation of daily independent practice time is an effective management tool. literacy center folders can be used to track which centers students have visited, as well as assess students' completion of the center and progress toward mastery.

Student accountability varies from recording responses extensively to a self-check or quick peer check with no written response at all. Since some activities have recording tasks built into them, while others do not, literacy center folders make management of student work easy.

Simply put, the literacy center folder is merely a receptacle for students' tracking sheets (if applicable) and activity recording sheets (if applicable). A literacy center folder is a folder or envelope, with a specific child's name on it, placed in a specific area of the classroom. Label these folders prominently with student names so that "filing" paperwork at the conclusion of each center is quick and easy.

One of the most efficient ways to house these large learning center folders in the classroom is with the use of rectangular, plastic laundry baskets. A portable, plastic filing cabinet also works well as a storage container.

These literacy center folders permit the teacher to look at each child as an individual, taking into consideration learning style, developmental stage, interests, and progress.

Teachers can then check the contents of folders daily or weekly to hold students accountable. The forms of assessment and the extent to which completion and correctness are "graded" is completely up to teacher discretion.

There are several things to consider when checking students' accountability and performance. The time when teachers themselves need to check student work for correctness is when students are being tested or checked for mastery. By then, the objective or skill being checked should have already been taught. After students have been given opportunities to practice and have had the opportunity to correct and learn from errors, it would be an appropriate time to assess. In other words, teachers should evaluate and "authentically assess" tests and one-on-one performance assignments, rather than daily practice work.

Sight Word Centers

300 Most Frequently Used Sight Words

Sight Word Cards*

Capture the Consonants

Fishing for Sight Words

Making Little Words

Concentration

Name Game

Newspaper Search

*Sight Word Cards can be used with a variety of centers.

Notes

300 Most Frequently Used Sight Words

Words 1–75

Words 1–25

the
of
and
a
to
in
is
you
that
it
he
was
for
on
are
as
with
his
they
I
at
be
this
have
from

Words 26–50

or
one
had
by
words
but
not
what
all
were
we
when
your
can
said
there
use
an
each
which
she
do
how
their
if

Words 51–75

will
up
other
about
out
many
then
them
these
so
some
her
would
make
like
him
into
time
has
look
two
more
write
go
see

300 Most Frequently Used Sight Words (cont.)

Words 76–150

Words 76–100	Words 101–125	Words 126–150
number	over	say
no	new	great
way	sound	where
could	take	help
people	only	through
my	little	much
than	work	before
first	know	line
water	place	right
been	years	too
call	live	means
who	me	old
am	back	any
its	give	same
now	most	tell
find	very	boy
long	after	following
down	things	came
day	our	want
did	just	show
get	name	also
come	good	around
made	sentence	farm
may	man	three
part	think	small

300 Most Frequently Used Sight Words *(cont.)*
Words 151–225

Words 151–175

set
put
end
does
another
well
large
must
big
even
such
because
turned
here
why
asked
went
men
read
need
land
different
home
us
move

Words 176–200

try
kind
hand
picture
again
change
off
play
spell
air
away
animals
house
point
page
letters
mother
answer
found
study
still
learn
should
American
world

Words 201–225

high
every
near
add
food
between
own
below
country
plants
last
school
father
keep
trees
never
started
city
earth
eyes
light
thought
head
under
story

300 Most Frequently Used Sight Words *(cont.)*
Words 226–300

Words 226–250	Words 251–275	Words 276–300
saw	important	miss
left	until	idea
don't	children	enough
few	side	eat
while	feet	face
along	car	watch
might	miles	far
close	night	Indians
something	walked	really
seemed	white	almost
next	sea	let
hard	began	above
open	grow	girl
example	took	sometimes
beginning	river	mountains
life	four	cut
always	carry	young
those	state	talk
both	once	soon
paper	book	list
together	hear	song
got	stop	being
group	without	leave
often	second	family
run	later	it's

the	he	at
of	was	be
and	for	this
a	on	have
to	are	from
in	as	or
is	with	one
you	his	had
that	they	by
it	I	words

Sight Words   Sight Words   Sight Words

Sight Words   Sight Words   Sight Words

Sight Words   Sight Words   Sight Words

Sight Words   Sight Words   Sight Words

Sight Words   Sight Words   Sight Words

Sight Words   Sight Words   Sight Words

Sight Words   Sight Words   Sight Words

Sight Words   Sight Words   Sight Words

Sight Words   Sight Words   Sight Words

Sight Words   Sight Words   Sight Words

but	there	will
not	use	up
what	an	other
all	each	about
were	which	out
we	she	many
when	do	then
your	how	them
can	their	these
said	if	so

Sight Words	Sight Words	Sight Words
Sight Words	Sight Words	Sight Words
Sight Words	Sight Words	Sight Words
Sight Words	Sight Words	Sight Words
Sight Words	Sight Words	Sight Words
Sight Words	Sight Words	Sight Words
Sight Words	Sight Words	Sight Words
Sight Words	Sight Words	Sight Words
Sight Words	Sight Words	Sight Words
Sight Words	Sight Words	Sight Words

some	two	my
her	more	than
would	write	first
make	go	water
like	see	been
him	number	call
into	no	who
time	way	am
has	could	its
look	people	now

Sight Words   Sight Words   Sight Words

Sight Words   Sight Words   Sight Words

Sight Words   Sight Words   Sight Words

Sight Words   Sight Words   Sight Words

Sight Words   Sight Words   Sight Words

Sight Words   Sight Words   Sight Words

Sight Words   Sight Words   Sight Words

Sight Words   Sight Words   Sight Words

Sight Words   Sight Words   Sight Words

find	over	years
long	new	live
down	sound	me
day	take	back
did	it's	give
get	only	most
come	little	very
made	work	after
may	know	things
part	place	our

Sight Words	**Sight Words**	**Sight Words**
Sight Words	**Sight Words**	**Sight Words**
Sight Words	**Sight Words**	**Sight Words**
Sight Words	**Sight Words**	**Sight Words**
Sight Words	**Sight Words**	**Sight Words**
Sight Words	**Sight Words**	**Sight Words**
Sight Words	**Sight Words**	**Sight Words**
Sight Words	**Sight Words**	**Sight Words**
Sight Words	**Sight Words**	**Sight Words**
Sight Words	**Sight Words**	**Sight Words**

just	through	tell
name	much	boy
good	before	following
sentence	line	came
man	right	want
think	too	show
say	means	also
great	old	around
where	any	farm
help	same	three

Sight Words   **Sight Words**   **Sight Words**

Sight Words   **Sight Words**   **Sight Words**

Sight Words   **Sight Words**   **Sight Words**

Sight Words   **Sight Words**   **Sight Words**

Sight Words   **Sight Words**   **Sight Words**

Sight Words   **Sight Words**   **Sight Words**

Sight Words   **Sight Words**   **Sight Words**

Sight Words   **Sight Words**   **Sight Words**

Sight Words   **Sight Words**   **Sight Words**

Sight Words   **Sight Words**   **Sight Words**

small	even	need
set	such	land
put	because	different
end	turned	home
does	here	us
another	why	move
well	asked	try
large	went	kind
must	men	hand
big	read	picture

Sight Words Sight Words Sight Words

Sight Words Sight Words Sight Words

Sight Words Sight Words Sight Words

Sight Words Sight Words Sight Words

Sight Words Sight Words Sight Words

Sight Words Sight Words Sight Words

Sight Words Sight Words Sight Words

Sight Words Sight Words Sight Words

Sight Words Sight Words Sight Words

Sight Words Sight Words Sight Words

again	page	world
change	letters	high
off	mother	every
play	answer	near
spell	found	add
air	study	food
away	still	between
animals	learn	own
house	should	below
point	American	country

Sight Words   Sight Words   Sight Words

Sight Words   Sight Words   Sight Words

Sight Words   Sight Words   Sight Words

Sight Words   Sight Words   Sight Words

Sight Words   Sight Words   Sight Words

Sight Words   Sight Words   Sight Words

Sight Words   Sight Words   Sight Words

Sight Words   Sight Words   Sight Words

Sight Words   Sight Words   Sight Words

Sight Words   Sight Words   Sight Words

plants	eyes	while
last	light	along
school	thought	might
father	head	close
keep	under	something
trees	story	seemed
never	saw	next
started	left	hard
city	don't	open
earth	few	example

Sight Words	Sight Words	Sight Words
Sight Words	Sight Words	Sight Words
Sight Words	Sight Words	Sight Words
Sight Words	Sight Words	Sight Words
Sight Words	Sight Words	Sight Words
Sight Words	Sight Words	Sight Words
Sight Words	Sight Words	Sight Words
Sight Words	Sight Words	Sight Words
Sight Words	Sight Words	Sight Words
Sight Words	Sight Words	Sight Words

beginning	run	white
life	important	sea
always	until	began
those	children	grow
both	side	took
paper	feet	river
together	car	four
got	miles	carry
group	night	state
often	walked	once

Sight Words	**Sight Words**	**Sight Words**
Sight Words	Sight Words	Sight Words
Sight Words	Sight Words	Sight Words
Sight Words	Sight Words	Sight Words
Sight Words	Sight Words	Sight Words
Sight Words	Sight Words	Sight Words
Sight Words	Sight Words	Sight Words
Sight Words	Sight Words	Sight Words
Sight Words	Sight Words	Sight Words
Sight Words	Sight Words	Sight Words

book	face	mountains
hear	watch	cut
stop	far	young
without	Indians	talk
second	really	soon
later	almost	list
miss	let	song
idea	above	being
enough	girl	leave
eat	sometimes	family

Sight Words	Sight Words	Sight Words
Sight Words	Sight Words	Sight Words
Sight Words	Sight Words	Sight Words
Sight Words	Sight Words	Sight Words
Sight Words	Sight Words	Sight Words
Sight Words	Sight Words	Sight Words
Sight Words	Sight Words	Sight Words
Sight Words	Sight Words	Sight Words
Sight Words	Sight Words	Sight Words
Sight Words	Sight Words	Sight Words

Capture the Consonants

Objective: Provides independent practice in the area of memorizing and writing sight words in addition to demonstrating knowledge of vowels and consonants.

What You Will Need

- Capture the Consonants recording sheet (page 46)
- paper
- list of sight words to be studied (pages 21–24)
- blue and green crayons or colored pencils

Create It

1. On a piece of paper or the class board, make a list of the sight words you would like your students to review.
2. Provide the above materials at a center.

Teach It

The center can be used continuously by changing the words to be studied. Students write sight words identifying the vowels and consonants within them. *Today we are going to write words and capture, or circle, the consonants with a blue writing tool. We will also capture, or underline, the vowels with a green writing tool. Let's say the vowels together: a, e, i, o, u.* Write a word to be studied on a piece of paper or the class board. Ask your students to identify which letters are consonants. Circle the consonants with a blue writing tool. With the green writing tool, underline the remaining vowels.

Do this lesson with your students until you are confident they are able to do the center independently.

Teacher Tip

- The vowels and consonants are simply to be identified—the activity is not sound related. Therefore, /y/ may be circled as a consonant on the recording sheet.

Keep in Mind: It can be difficult for young children to distinguish between vowels and consonants. Practice saying the vowel letters out loud throughout the day. For example, practice saying the vowels while standing in line.

Extension Ideas

- Use weekly spelling lists instead of sight words.
- Modify the number of words to be written.

Home Connection: Have students do this activity as homework with the names of family members.

Capture the Consonants

Directions: Write your name. Use a blue crayon to capture (circle) the consonants.

My name is

Directions: Record your words below. Capture (circle) the consonants using a blue crayon. Underline the vowels with a green crayon.

Capture the Consonants

flower

f l o w e r

1. Write your name on the recording sheet.

2. Circle the consonants with the blue crayon.

3. Underline the vowels with the green crayon.

4. Read the first word on the list.

5. Write the word on your recording sheet.

6. Circle consonants with the blue crayon.

7. Underline vowels with the green crayon.

8. Do all of the words on your list.

Fishing for Sight Words

Objective: Provides independent practice in the area of reading sight words.

What You Will Need
- Fish Sight Word Cards (page 53)
- small dowel or pointer to be used as fishing pole
- string, approximately one yard (one meter)
- magnet
- paper clips
- bucket or large bowl
- Optional: recording sheet (page 50)

Create It
1. Cut the Fish Sight Word Cards apart or create your own fish cards by using the blank fish template on page 55.
2. Create a fishing pole by tying the string around the dowel and attaching the magnet at the end of the string.
3. Affix a paper clip to each fish card.
4. Place the fish in a bucket or large bowl in the middle of the center.

Teach It
The center can be used continuously by changing the words to be studied. Students read words they "fish" out of a bucket or tub. *Today we are going to fish for words.* Demonstrate for the students how to carefully drop the magnet end of the string into the bucket or bowl, and then slowly bring the line back out. Set the fishing pole down and remove the fish from the magnet. Read the words out loud to your students. Place the words back into the bucket and the next player takes a turn. Ask students to demonstrate the activity by taking turns in front of the class. Do this lesson with your students until you are confident they are able to do the center independently. If appropriate, have students record their "catches" on the recording sheet.

Teacher Tip
- A "pond" could be created with blue construction paper, a baby bathtub or small wading pool.

Keep in Mind: The "fishing pole" could be dangerous in the hands of some children. Spend time with your students discussing the proper way to hold and use the fishing pole.

Extension Ideas
- Use weekly spelling, vocabulary, or thematic word lists instead of sight words.
- Modify the number of words to be fished.

Home Connection: As a homework activity, have students practice reading the sight words they recorded on the recording sheet. Then, ask your students to use the words in a sentence.

Fishing for Sight Words

Words I Caught!

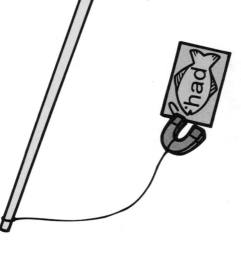

Fishing for Sight Words

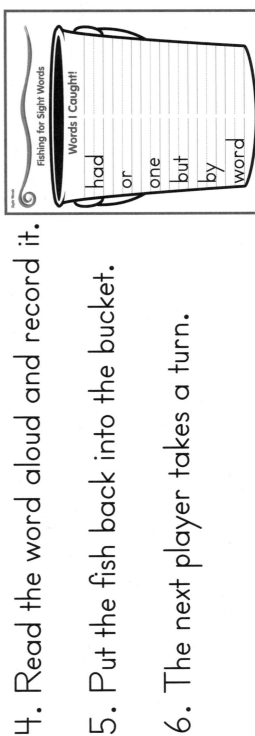

Fishing for Sight Words

Words I Caught!

| had |
| or |
| one |
| but |
| by |
| word |

1. Go fishing.

2. Catch a fish.

3. Set the pole down and take the fish off.

4. Read the word aloud and record it.

5. Put the fish back into the bucket.

6. The next player takes a turn.

Fishing for Sight Words

Fish Sight Word Cards

Fishing
for
Sight Words

Fishing
for
Sight Words

Fishing
for
Sight Words

Fishing
for
Sight Words

Fishing
for
Sight Words

Fishing
for
Sight Words

Fishing for Sight Words

Blank Sight Words Cards

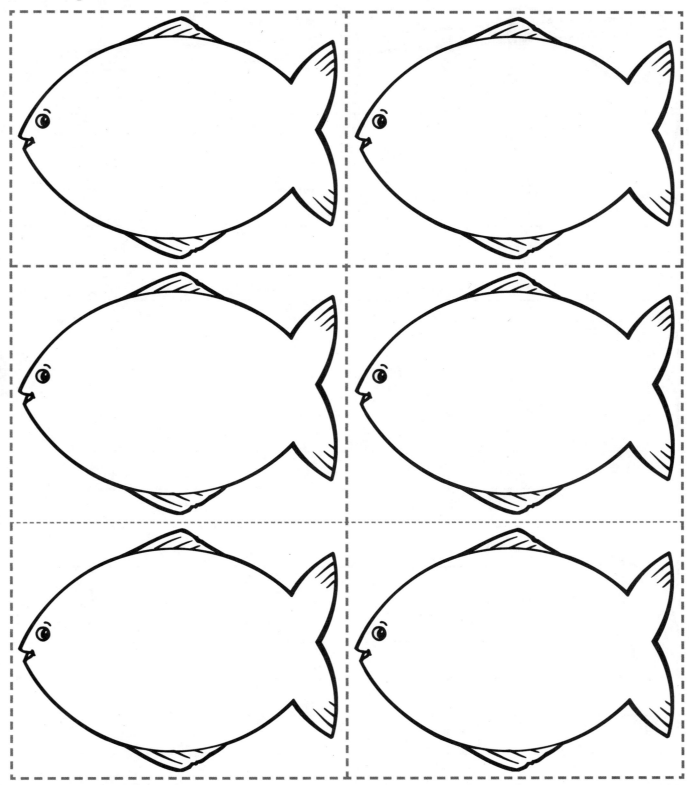

Fishing for Sight Words

Directions: Use the words that you "caught" in sentences. Underline the words.

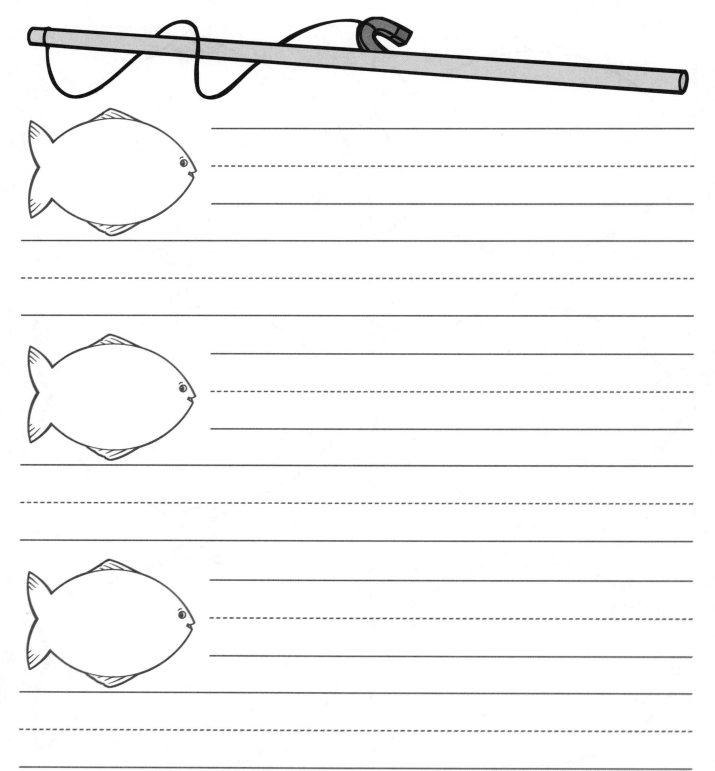

Making Little Words

Objective: Provides independent practice in the area of reading and creating sight words.

What You Will Need

- Making Little Words grid paper (page 58)
- teacher-chosen sight words (pages 21–24) or sight word cards
- pencils
- scissors

Create It

1. Provide students with pencils, scissors, and Making Little Words grid paper.
2. On a large piece of paper, write sight words for your students to practice spelling.

Teach It

The center can be used continuously by changing the words to be studied. Students find smaller words using the letters in the larger words.

Today we are going to create little words using the letters in our sight word. Show the students how to write a sight word in the boxes of the grid paper on page 58. *First, we need to choose a sight word from the list or pick a sight word card. Then, we write the sight word on the grid paper, putting each letter in its own box. Then we will cut the boxes apart.* Demonstrate for students how to write the uppercase version of each letter on the back side of each letter card once it has been cut apart. As a class, see how many little words you can create using the letters you have cut out. Have students manipulate the cards to create the words. Do this lesson with your students until you are confident they are able to do the center independently.

Teacher Tips

- Use sight words that are at least four letters long.
- Emphasize that each letter must be written correctly.
- Instead of a list of sight words, use several of the sight word flash cards from the beginning of the Sight Words section.

Keep in Mind: Combining letters from different words will enable children to make more and more words.

Extension Ideas

- Use the names of children in the class, or thematic or holiday words as key words.
- Have children use a recording sheet to record little words. Do not provide them with a list of words to create.

Home Connection: Have students do this activity at home using family members names. Have students make a list of words they were able to create.

Making Little Words

Grid Paper

Making Little Words

1. Write the letters for the sight word in the boxes grid paper.

2. Cut the boxes, or grid, apart.

3. Write the uppercase letters on the backs of the cards.

4. Create new words using the letter cards.

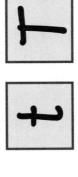

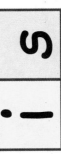

Concentration

Objective: Provides independent practice in the area of reading instant sight words while improving memorization skills.

What You Will Need

- Sight Word Concentration Cards (pages 65-68)

Create It

1. Cut out the concentration cards to be used during center time.
2. Make additional cards as needed using the blank cards. (page 62)
3. Laminate the cards and arrange a card-playing area.

Teach It

The center can be used continuously by changing the words to be studied. Students find matching sight words. *Today we are going to play a card game called Concentration.* Demonstrate to the students how to shuffle the cards and then lay the cards out face down, in rows. Ask for volunteers to take turns coming up and turning over two cards. If he or she finds a pair, then he or she gets to keep the cards. If the two cards do not match, the cards are turned back over and another player takes a turn.

Do this lesson with your students until you are confident they are able to do the center independently.

Teacher Tip

- If more cards are desired, make an extra set of sight word cards for your students to use. Index cards would work well.

Keep in Mind: The game could get competitive. Encourage children to play fairly. This game could be played independently as well.

Extension Idea

- Use the blank template on page 62 to create additional cards. Use weekly spelling, vocabulary, or thematic word lists instead of sight words.

Home Connection: Have students play this game at home using cards they make themselves, or a regular deck of playing cards, to practice number identification and memorization skills.

Concentration

Blank Sight Word Concentration Cards

Concentration

Sight Word Concentration	Sight Word Concentration	Sight Word Concentration
Sight Word Concentration	**last**	Sight Word Concentration
Sight Word Concentration	Sight Word Concentration	Sight Word Concentration
last	Sight Word Concentration	Sight Word Concentration

1. Shuffle the cards.

2. Lay them on the table face down in rows.

3. Turn over two cards.

4. If the cards match, keep them. If the cards do not match, turn them back over.

5. The next player takes a turn.

Concentration

Sight Word Concentration Cards

high	**high**
every	**every**
near	**near**

Sight Word Concentration

Sight Word Concentration

Sight Word Concentration

Sight Word Concentration

Sight Word Concentration

Sight Word Concentration

Concentration

Sight Word Concentration Cards *(cont.)*

plant	plant
last	last
school	school

Sight Word Concentration

Sight Word Concentration

Sight Word Concentration

Sight Word Concentration

Sight Word Concentration

Sight Word Concentration

Name Game

Objective: Provides independent practice in the area of writing and utilizing sight words.

What You Will Need

- Name Cards for each student (page 70)
- selected Sight Word Cards (pages 25–44)
- Name Game recording sheet(s) (pages 73–74)
- lined writing paper

Jaden

Create It

1. Write the names of the children in the classroom on the Name Cards (page 70). Don't forget to include your own name.
2. Choose Sight Word Cards you wish to use.
3. Provide Name Game recording sheets or lined writing paper and pencils in the center.

Teach It

Children use their classmates' names in sentences they construct. *Today we are going to write sentences using our classmates' names and our sight words. First we will choose a name card and a sight word card. Then, we will read the sight word and the name we have chosen. Finally, we will write a sentence using the name and sight word.* Select a child's name and place it where everyone can read it. Select a sight word and show the children the word. With the class, do a shared writing by creating a sentence that incorporates both of the words. *After you have written the first sentence, choose four more name cards and four more sight word cards.* Encourage the children to help you create four more sentences using the remaining Sight Word Cards and Name Cards. Do this lesson with your students until you are confident they are able to do the center independently.

Teacher Tips

- Review both sets of cards with students before center time.

Keep in Mind: Remember to think about the level of your "spellers" as you are deciding which sight words to use.

Extension Ideas

- Use weekly spelling lists instead of sight words.
- Have children write only "non-fiction" sentences.
- Use more than one name or sight word in a sentence.

fly

Home Connection: Using the Name Game recording sheet on page 74, have students use their family members' names and sight words in sentences. Encourage your students to write a short story.

Name Game

Student Name Cards or Sight Word Cards

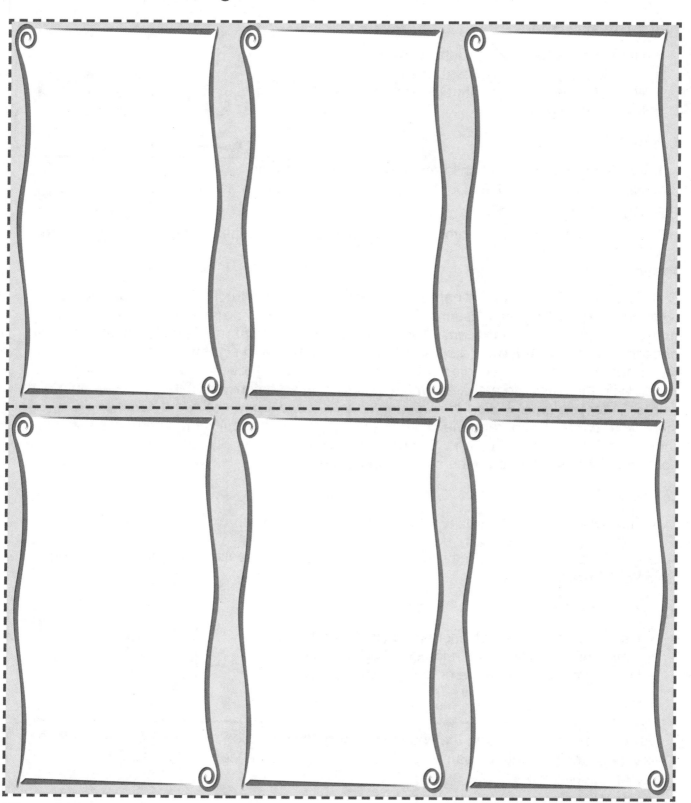

Nancy

time

Name Game

Directions: Write a sentence using the name and the sight word you chose.

Classmate's Name — Nancy

Sight Word — time

Nancy came home on time.

Name Game

1. Select and read one Sight Word Card and one Name Card.

2. Read each card.

3. Think of a sentence using the name on the card and the sight word.

4. Write your sentence on your paper.

5. Do this activity for each sight word.

Name Game

Directions: Write a sentence using the name and the sight word you chose.

Classmate's Name _____   Sight Word _____

_____

_____

_____

_____

Name Game

Directions: Write a sentence using the name and the sight word you chose.

Classmate's Name _____   Sight Word _____

_____

_____

_____

_____

Name Game

Directions: Use your family members' names, and the same number of sight words, to write sentences or a short story.

Newspaper Search

Objective: Provides independent practice in the area of reading instant sight words.

What You Will Need

1. newspaper article or weekly periodical for each participant
2. Sight Word Cards or other word cards
3. highlighter pens for each participant
4. overhead transparency, pen, and projector, index cards

Create It

1. Cut several articles out of the newspaper.
2. Select and display five Sight Word Cards for which to search (pages 25–44), or make new sight words using index cards.

Teach It

This center can be used continuously by changing the words to be studied. Students locate given words in provided text. Prior to doing a lesson, copy an article onto an overhead transparency sheet. Display the article in the classroom so that the children are able to read it. Explain to the students: *Today we are going to search for our sight words in newspaper articles. We are going to look through the article for these five words.* Display the words so that all of the children can see them. *We are going to use a highlighter pen to hightlight words when we find them.* Demonstrate to the students, using your overhead copy and an overhead pen, how to highlight the given words. *Search for the first word on the list. Highlight all of the places where you find it. Do this activity one word at a time.* Do this lesson with your students until you are confident that they are able to do the center procedures independently.

Teacher Tips

- Newspaper print is small. Enlarge the article for younger students.
- It is much easier for students if they look for one word at a time.

Keep in Mind: Highlighter and overhead markers can stain clothing.

Extension Ideas

- Copy the article several times to allow many students to use the same article.
- Modify the task by writing the number of times the words can be found in a particular article at the top of the page.
- Laminate the articles and have students use an overhead marker to note where the words have been found. Then the child can simply erase the page for the next student.
- After locating the words, have students use the words in a sentence.

Home Connection: Have students work with their family members to highlight words from a list you have provided in articles that they have at home.

Newspaper Search

The students were not going to have their class picnic on Saturday.

The principal said they had to wait for better weather.

said

not

words

have

they

1. Read the word cards.

2. Search for the words needed.

3. Look for one word at a time.

4. Highlight each word as you find it.

Phonics and Decoding Centers

Alphabet Soup

Categories

Labels, Labels, Labels

Partner Reading

Pick-a-Word

Use the Clues

Notes

Alphabet Soup

Objective: Provides independent practice in the area of letter recognition and sound identification.

What You Will Need

- plastic soda or water bottle lids or poker chips
- bowl or pot
- markers
- ladle
- Alphabet Soup recording sheet (page 82)

Create It

1. Write the letters to be studied in both uppercase and lowercase on the bottle lids or poker chips. Use a permanent marker.
2. Place the lids or chips in the container and the ladle in the center.

Teach It

Today we are going to use this ladle to scoop out a few letters from the bowl (pot) of alphabet soup. Have a volunteer come up and ladle out one of the letters in the bowl. *Boys and girls, what is this letter?* Give students an opportunity to respond. *What sound does this letter make?* After children respond, demonstrate how to write the letter in one of the boxes on a recording sheet and then write words that start with the same letter sound. *Take turns scooping out two caps. Write one letter in each bowl on the recording sheet. Then write some words that begin with each letter.*

Do this lesson with your students until you are confident that they are able to do the center procedures independently.

Teacher Tip

- Remind students to scoop out one or two chips (or caps) at a time.

Extension Idea

- Have students draw a picture that begins with the letter they chose. (Example: a cat, dog, dish, car, apple, etc.)

Home Connection: Have students say the sounds of the letters as they eat alphabet soup or alphabet shaped cereal at home.

Alphabet Soup

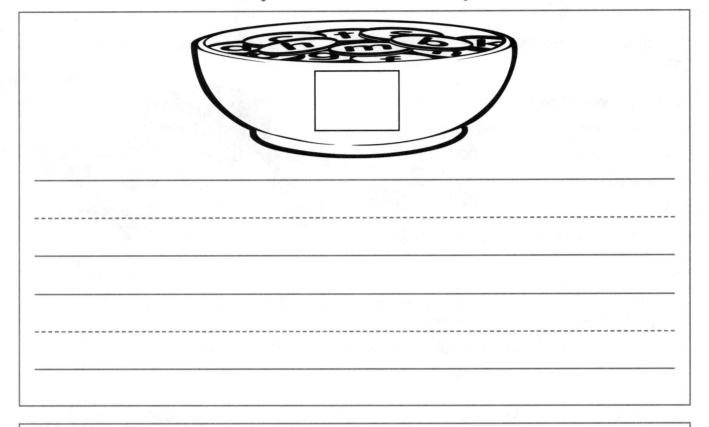

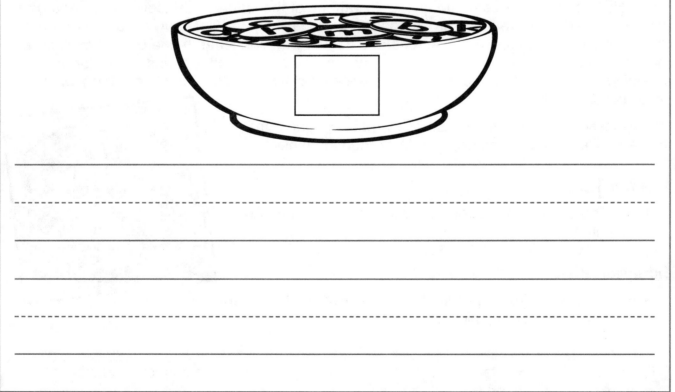

Alphabet Soup

bat

boy

1. Use the ladle to scoop out caps.

2. Write the letters of 2 of the caps in the boxes on the bowls.

3. Write 2 words that begin with each letter.

b-a-t   b-o-y   h-a-t   h-o-m-e

4. Write a sentence using some of the words you wrote.

The boy put on his hat.

Categories

Objective: Provides independent practice in the area of spelling words and categorizing items.

What You Will Need

- Categories recording sheet (page 86)
- Category Cards (page 89)
- Consonant Cards (page 91)
- pencils

Create It

1. Cut apart the Category and Consonant Cards.
2. Provide the above items in a center.

Teach It

Today we are going to play Categories. I am choosing two Category Cards from this stack and two Letter or Consonant Cards from this stack. On the board, create a table that looks like the student recording sheet for this activity. Write the two different category names in the boxes across the top and the two different letters in the boxes going down the side. Have your students volunteer ideas that will fit in each category. For example, if the first category is "Things That Fly" and the first letter chosen is B, someone might suggest *bird*. Continue demonstrating the activity until all of the boxes are filled. Do this lesson with your students until you are confident they are able to do the center independently.

Teacher Tips

- Be sure the categories you chose are ones that the students can easily identify.
- Have children select a new Consonant Card when one is chosen that is too difficult.

Keep in Mind: Some students may be able to work with more challenging words or categories. Provide a large variety of categories and words for your students to work with.

Extension Idea

- Add sounds or categories to be worked on.

Home Connection: Have students do this activity at home with family members by brainstorming together a particular activity and all of the items that will fall into that category that start with a particular letter.

Categories

Name _____

Beginning Sounds

Beginning Sounds

Categories

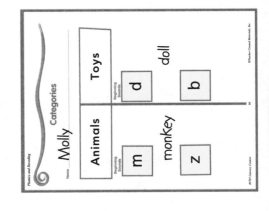

1. Choose two Category Cards.

2. Write a category in each box at the top of the page.

3. Choose two Consonant Cards.

4. Write the consonants in the two small boxes.

5. Write a word under each category that begins with the specific sound.

Category Cards

Foods	Sports
Things That Fly	Stores
Animals	Toys
Places	Restaurants
Birds	Clothes
Vehicles	Games

Categories

Consonant Cards

b	c	d	f	g
h	j	k	l	m
n	p	q	r	s
t	v	w	x	y
z	th	ch	sh	wh

Consonants	Consonants	Consonants	Consonants	Consonants
Consonants	Consonants	Consonants	Consonants	Consonants
Consonants	Consonants	Consonants	Consonants	Consonants
Consonants	Consonants	Consonants	Consonants	Consonants
Consonants	Consonants	Consonants	Consonants	Consonants

Labels, Labels, Labels

Objective: Provides independent practice in the area of word decoding and phonics by labeling pictures of known items.

What You Will Need

- recording sheet (page 94)
- Picture Cards (pages 97–104)
- pencils
- Word Card Labels (pages 105–108)
- bags or containers

Create It

1. Cut apart the Picture Cards and Word Card Labels (pages 97–104).
2. Place each card and it;s matching label cards in a seperate bag or container.

Teach It

Today we are going to label pictures. Remember when we are spelling words, it is very important to listen to every sound we hear in the word and write down all of the sounds that are heard. Also, remember the rules of spelling we have learned so far. (Such as the long vowel rules, etc.) Demonstrate to students how everything in the pictures can be labeled. Demonstrate how even one item (such as tree) can be labeled even further. *For example, when we label a tree, we could label the leaf, branch, trunk, bark, etc.*

Do this lesson with your students until you are confident they are able to do the center independently.

Teacher Tip

- Accept invented spelling for additional words children might supply. The primary focus is on sounds, especially beginning and ending sounds.

Keep in Mind: Students may need to be reminded to label the details in the picture.

Extension Ideas

- Cut out new pictures from magazines, glue them to a piece of tag paper, and laminate them. Encourge children to listen for beginning and ending sounds when writing new words (labels).

- Use the Word Card Labels (pages 105–108) to help your students extend their vocabulary.

Home Connection: Have student draw a picture of his or her bedroom. Instruct students to label their drawings.

Labels, Labels, Labels

Name _____

Picture Number

Name _____

Picture Number

Labels, Labels, Labels

1. Select a picture to label.

2. Use the matching Word Card Labels.

table	sun	boy

3. Fill in the recording page. Write the number of the picture on the recording sheet.

4. List the labels you used on the recording sheet.

Name ___Cole___

4
Picture Number

table

boy

sun

Labels
Labels
Labels

Labels
Labels
Labels

Labels

Labels

Labels

Labels

Labels

Labels

5.

6.

Labels
Labels
Labels

Labels
Labels
Labels

7.

8.

Labels

Labels

Labels

Labels

Labels

Labels

Labels, Labels, Labels

Word Card Labels

flowers	swing	cow	calf
bunny	grass	sheep	lamb
sun	tree	chicken	chick
sand	beach	table	cook
ball	boat	boy	chips
shovel	bucket	sun	forks

Labels

Labels	**Labels**	**Labels**	**Labels**
Card 2	Card 2	Card 1	Card 1
Labels	**Labels**	**Labels**	**Labels**
Card 2	Card 2	Card 1	Card 1
Labels	**Labels**	**Labels**	**Labels**
Card 2	Card 2	Card 1	Card 1
Labels	**Labels**	**Labels**	**Labels**
Card 4	Card 4	Card 3	Card 3
Labels	**Labels**	**Labels**	**Labels**
Card 4	Card 4	Card 3	Card 3
Labels	**Labels**	**Labels**	**Labels**
Card 4	Card 4	Card 3	Card 3

Labels, Labels, Labels

Word Card Labels *(cont.)*

bird	rake	pumpkin	stars
leaf	apple	jack -o- lantern	costume
ball	child	candy	parent
cloud	jacket	house	snow
mittens	hat	boots	snowman
skis	ski poles	gloves	scarf

Labels

Labels Card 6	**Labels** Card 6	**Labels** Card 5	**Labels** Card 5
Labels Card 6	**Labels** Card 6	**Labels** Card 5	**Labels** Card 5
Labels Card 6	**Labels** Card 6	**Labels** Card 5	**Labels** Card 5
Labels Card 8	**Labels** Card 8	**Labels** Card 7	**Labels** Card 7
Labels Card 8	**Labels** Card 8	**Labels** Card 7	**Labels** Card 7
Labels Card 8	**Labels** Card 8	**Labels** Card 7	**Labels** Card 7

Partner Reading

Objective: Provides independent reading practice.

What You Will Need

- short, decodable, easy readers
- Partner Reading recording sheet (page 110)

Create It

1. Establish a comfortable area where partners can go to read.
2. Arrange an area for students to complete the recording sheet after taking turns reading, if appropriate.

Teach It

Students will read to their peers. *Today we are going to read to each other. Each of you is going to pick a partner. One partner will listen while the other reads. The listener's job will be to listen and provide help with any words the partner might struggle with.* It is important to practice this activity to reinforce listening skills and taking turns. Do this lesson with your students until you are confident they are able to do the center independently.

Teacher Tip

- Encourage students to choose books they have already read in class. Short, decodable books provided in many language arts series are perfect for this activity.

Keep in Mind: It is sometimes helpful to pair children of different abilities—a good reader paired with a reader who is just learning.

Extension Idea

- After your students have read their books with their partner, have them illustrate a picture about their favorite part of each story. Use the Partner Reading recording sheet on page 110.

Home Connection: Have students read to family members at home.

Partner Reading

Title: _____

_____

_____

Author: _____

_____

My favorite part was:

_____

_____

_____

_____

_____

Draw a picture of your favorite part.

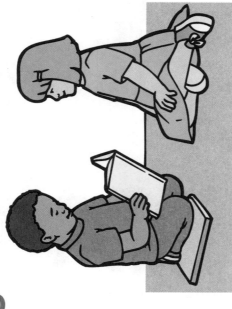

Partner Reading

1. Read to a friend.

2. Take turns being a good listener.

3. Talk about your book with your partner.

Optional: Fill in the recording sheet.

Pick-a-Word

Objective: Provides independent practice in the area of blending onsets and rimes.

What You Will Need

- Onset and Rime Cards (pages 117–128)
- two small buckets or containers
- Pick-a-Word recording sheet (page 114)

Create It

1. Cut apart the Onset and Rime Cards.
2. Put the Onset and Rime Cards in separate, small buckets.

Teach It

Today we are going to play a game called Pick-a-Word. I need a volunteer to choose an Onset Card from one bucket and choose a Rime Card from the other bucket. After the student has chosen the specific cards, have classroom volunteers help blend the initial consonant sound with the ending rime. Write the word created on the board. If the two cards, when blended together, do not make a real word, pick new cards.

Do this lesson with your students until you are confident they are able to do the center independently.

Teacher Tips

- Try to use initial consonants that will make words with most, if not all, of the rimes listed on the other box.
- Be careful to check that inappropriate words cannot be created by any combination of the cards picked.
- Remind your students that the *onset* is the initial sound, and the *rime* is the ending of the word.

Keep in Mind: The term *onset* simply indicates the initial sound of a word. The *rime* is the pattern of sound (starting with the vowel sound) that follows. For example, when using the word *back*, the onset is /b/ and the rime is /ack/.

Extension Idea

- Have students list other words that can be made using the rime pattern that was picked.

Home Connection: Have students make a list of words that belong in a particular rime family.

wig — pig
jig — ig — dig
fig — twig

Pick-a-Word

Directions: Pick an Onset Card and a Rime Card. If a word is formed, write it on the lines provided on your recording page. Use the word in a sentence.

onset   rime   word

Pick-a-Word

Directions: Pick an Onset Card and a Rime Card. If a word is formed, write it on the lines provided on your recording page. Use the word in a sentence.

onset   rime   word

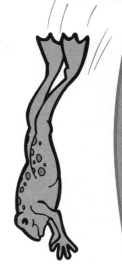

Pick-a-Word

1. Pick an Onset Card and a Rime Card.

2. Blend the sound of the Onset Card with the Rime Card.

3. If the cards make a real word, write it on your paper. If a real word cannot be made, pick again.

4. Use your word in a sentence.

fr-og

The frog hopped!

Onset Cards

b	c	d
f	g	h
j	k	l
m	n	p
r	s	t

Onset Cards

Onset Cards	**Onset Cards**	**Onset Cards**
Onset Cards	**Onset Cards**	**Onset Cards**
Onset Cards	**Onset Cards**	**Onset Cards**
Onset Cards	**Onset Cards**	**Onset Cards**
Onset Cards	**Onset Cards**	**Onset Cards**

Onset Cards

v	w	x
y	z	bl
br	ch	cl
cr	dr	fl
fr	gl	pl

Onset Cards

Onset Cards	**Onset Cards**	**Onset Cards**
Onset Cards	**Onset Cards**	**Onset Cards**
Onset Cards	**Onset Cards**	**Onset Cards**
Onset Cards	**Onset Cards**	**Onset Cards**
Onset Cards	**Onset Cards**	**Onset Cards**

Onset Cards

kn	qu	sh
sl	sn	sp
th	tr	wr
spr	str	st

Onset Cards

Onset Cards	**Onset Cards**	**Onset Cards**
Onset Cards	**Onset Cards**	**Onset Cards**
Onset Cards	**Onset Cards**	**Onset Cards**
Onset Cards	**Onset Cards**	**Onset Cards**
Onset Cards	**Onset Cards**	**Onset Cards**

Rime Cards

ag	am	an
ap	at	ed
en	est	et
id	ig	ill
in	ing	ink

Rime Cards

Rime
Cards

Rime
Cards

Rime
Cards

Rime
Cards

Rime
Cards

Rime
Cards

Rime
Cards

Rime
Cards

Rime
Cards

Rime
Cards

Rime
Cards

Rime
Cards

Rime
Cards

Rime
Cards

Rime
Cards

Rime Cards

ip	it	ock
og	op	ot
ub	uck	ug
um	un	ut
ail	ain	ake

Rime Cards

Rime Cards   **Rime Cards**   **Rime Cards**

Rime Cards   **Rime Cards**   **Rime Cards**

Rime Cards   **Rime Cards**   **Rime Cards**

Rime Cards   **Rime Cards**   **Rime Cards**

Rime Cards   **Rime Cards**   **Rime Cards**

Rime Cards

ame	ank	ate
eat	eep	ice
ide	ime	ive
oat	old	ole
one	ose	y

Rime Cards

Rime Cards	**Rime Cards**	**Rime Cards**
Rime Cards	**Rime Cards**	**Rime Cards**
Rime Cards	**Rime Cards**	**Rime Cards**
Rime Cards	**Rime Cards**	**Rime Cards**
Rime Cards	**Rime Cards**	**Rime Cards**

Use the Clues

Objective: Provides independent practice in the area of reading by using the context clues provided in the sentences.

What You Will Need

- Use the Clues recording sheet (page 130)
- overhead markers
- Sentence Strips (pages 133–140)
- wet wipes and tissues
- pencils

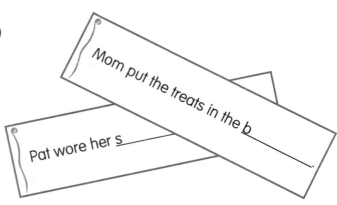

Create It

1. Cut out and laminate the sentence strips.
2. Provide the items noted above in a center.

Teach It

This activity builds phonics and decoding ability through spelling. *Today we are going to complete sentences that are missing words, by reading the clues. We will use the words around the missing word, and the beginning sound, as clues.* Read an example sentence and write it on the board. "(Patty wore her s _____." *Could I put the word "car" on the line to finish the word that begins with the letter "S"? No, car starts with c and not s. Also, because you cannot wear a car.* Discuss with your students how to look at the clues to help figure out what the word might be. *The word is obviously something a girl could wear and it begins with the letter s.* Have students brainstorm a list of things the word could be. *For example, the word could be scarf, skirt, or slippers.* Model for your student how to write the word in the blank provided. Do this lesson with your students until you are confident they are able to do the center independently.

Teacher Tip

- If students are going to write directly on the laminated strips, use a tissue to dry the Sentence Strip after cleaning it with a wet wipe.

Keep in Mind: Your students' answers will vary for this activity.

Extension Ideas

- Vary the number of responses necessary for each sentence.
- Create your own Sentence Strips by using blank Sentence Strips or pieces of construction paper. Use sentences from new stories to introduce new vocabulary words.

Home Connection: Have student create his or her own sentence having a missing word that begins with a certain sound. Have family members create a list of possible answers.

Use the Clues

Directions: Record the two words you might use to fill in the blank. Choose one word and write the sentence.

Possible Words

_____   _____

- - - - - - - - - - - - - - - - - - -   -

_____   _____

Sentence

_____

- -

_____

_____

_____

- -

Use the Clues

Directions: Record the two words you might use to fill in the blank. Choose one word and write the sentence.

Possible Words

_____   _____

- - - - - - - - - - - - - - - - - - -   -

_____   _____

Sentence

_____

- -

_____

_____

- -

Use the Clues

I drove my car to the d_____.

doctor
dance
dentist

1. Choose a sentence strip and read the sentence. Use the beginning sound of the missing word as a clue.

2. Think of words to finish the sentence.

3. Record two words on the sheet.

4. Choose one of the words and write a sentence.

5. Read your sentence out loud.

Use the Clues

Directions: Record the words you used to finish the sentences.

Possible Words

doctor	dance

Sentence

I drove my car to the dance.

Use the Clues Sentences

Pat wore her s _____.

We will d _____ at the party!

Mom put the treats in the b _____.

Sentence Strip Cards

Sentence Strip Cards

Sentence Strip Cards

Use the Clues Sentences *(cont.)*

Look! There's a f _____
in our bathtub.

I wrote my name on my b _____ .

I wish my mom could come to the
p _____ .

Sentence Strip Cards

Sentence Strip Cards

Sentence Strip Cards

Use the Clues Sentences *(cont.)*

We went s _____ after the game.

Do you want to help me clean the d _____ ?

I drove my car to the d _____ .

Sentence Strip Cards

Sentence Strip Cards

Sentence Strip Cards

Use the Clues Sentences *(cont.)*

I like to play s _____.

I don't like to eat s _____.

I am good at r _____.

Sentence Strip Cards

Sentence Strip Cards

Sentence Strip Cards

Reading and Writing Response Centers

Ask the Author

Blooming Questions

Book Talk

Convince Me

Would You Rather?

Retell the Story

Notes

Ask the Author

Objective: Provides independent practice in the area of reading, writing, and reasoning.

What You Will Need

- any text
- lined paper
- pencils
- Ask the Author recording sheets (pages 144, and 148)

Create It

1. Provide the items listed above at a center.

2. Display the Ask the Author letter writing poster (page 147) in a prominant location.

Teach It

Students create a list of questions they would like to ask the author of a book they have read. Model this activity by doing it with the students. Read a story together. Ask for volunteers to suggest questions they would like to ask the author, or person who wrote the book. For example: *Why did you choose the character you wrote about? Do you know anyone like the main character? Is he or she based on someone you know? Did this ever happen to you? Do the pictures in the story look like the pictures you had in your mind when you wrote the story?* Record these questions on the Ask the Author recording sheet (page 144). Discuss your favorite part of the story with your students. Using page 148 as a guide, draw a new cover for your book and display it in the classroom for all to see. Do this lesson with your students until you are confident they are able to do the center independently.

Teacher Tips

- Use books that have a simple storyline so your students are able to comprehend the entire story.
- Some students would rather draw a picture of their favorite part.
  You may want to use the recording sheet on page 148 for these students.

Keep in Mind: Picture books work well for this activity.

Extension Idea

- Have students write a letter to the author and ask a question, or make comments about the book. Use the poster on page 147 as a guide.

Home Connection: Have students write five questions they would like to ask the writer(s) of their favorite TV program.

Ask the Author

Name: _____

Book title: _____

Author: _____

Directions: Write three questions you would like to ask the author.

1. _____

_____

_____

2. _____

_____

_____

3. _____

_____

_____

Reading and Writing Response

Ask the Author

Name: Samantha
Book title: Life in the Jungle
Author: Liz Ely
Directions: Write three questions you would like to ask the author.

1. Is it scary in the Jungle ?

2.

3.

#3703 Literacy Centers for Reading Skills (K–2)   144   ©Teacher Created Materials, Inc.

Ask the Author

1. Read the story.

2. Write three questions you would like to ask the author about the book.

3. Draw a new cover for the book to make other children want to read it.

Ask the Author

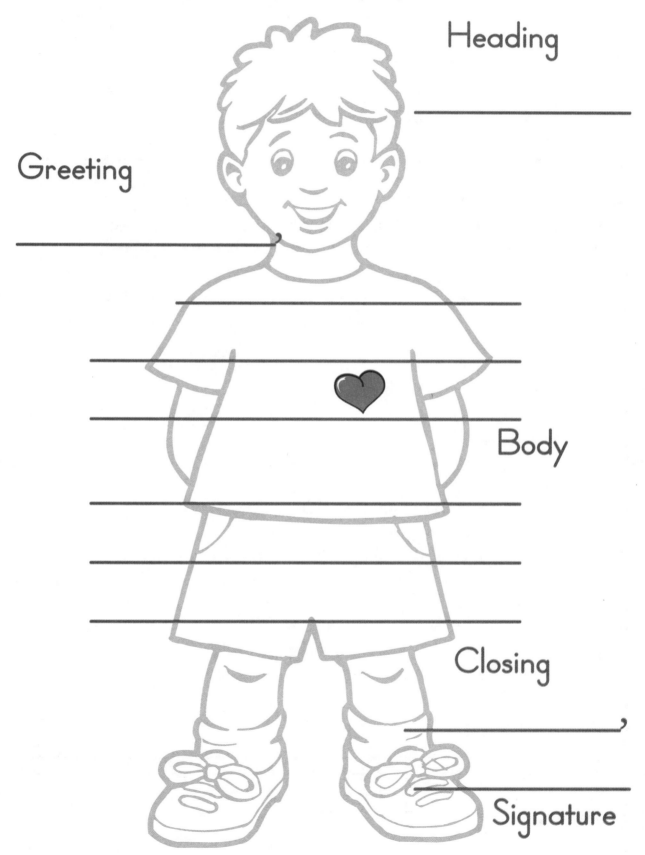

Heading

Greeting

Body

Closing

Signature

Ask the Author

Title: -

Author: -

Directions: Draw a new cover for your book in the space below.

Name: -

Blooming Questions

Objective: Provides independent practice in the areas of reading, comprehension, and writing.

What You Will Need

- Blooming Questions recording sheet (page 150)
- writing sample or book
- pencils

Create It

1. Find an appropriate book or student writing sample to share.
2. Copy the Blooming Questions recording sheet onto a transparency.

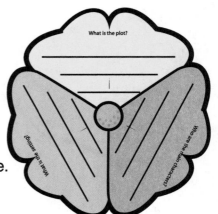

Teach It

Students will respond to questions about a piece of writing they have read. Display the transparancy on an overhead. *Today we are going to listen to a story (article) and then answer questions about it. Is everyone ready? Let's review the questions on our Blooming Questions sheet.* Read a piece of writing with students. With the assistance of student volunteers, complete the form. Spend time on each question, making sure students are familiar with the terms.

Do this lesson with your students until you are confident that they are able to do the center procedures independently.

Teacher Tip

- Review the parts of a story with students before having them do this center.

Extension Ideas

- Draw pictures in response to each question.
- Create a flower template with more petals and more questions.

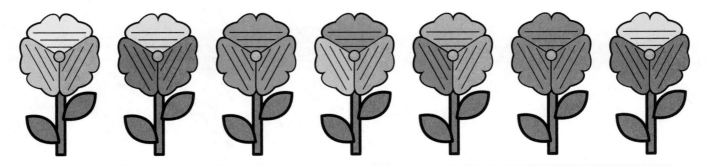

Home Connection: Have students use the Blooming Questions recording sheet as a book report for a homework assignment.

Blooming Questions

Name: _____

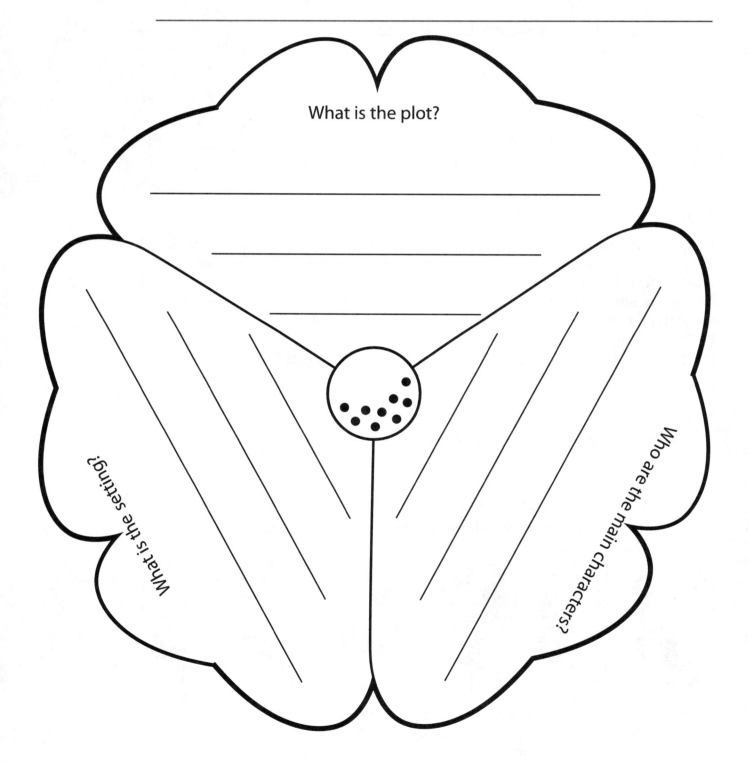

What is the plot?

_____

_____

_____

What is the setting?

Who are the main characters?

Blooming Questions

Reading and Writing Response

Blooming Questions

Name: _____

Who are the main characters?

What is the plot?

What is the setting?

#3703 Literacy Centers for Reading Skills (K–2)   150   ©Teacher Created Materials, Inc.

1. Read a book or article.

2. Read the questions on the flower.

3. Write your answers to the questions.

4. Color the flower.

Book Talk

Objective: Provides independent practice in reading, comprehension, and verbal expression.

What You Will Need

- copy of previously read book or article
- Optional: Book Talk recording sheet (page 154)

Create It

1. Provide the items noted above at a center.

Teach It

Model a "book talk" for your students. Explain that they will be talking with a partner about books they have read. After reading a book together in class, hold an open discussion about the text. Have students talk about the parts they liked, and the parts they disliked. Model, for your students, how to be a good listener. Brainstorm questions to ask the reader about the book. For example: *What was your favorite part? What was the conflict and how was it resolved? Who was the main character? What other books did this author write?* Encourage students to ask each other questions about the story using positive language. Do this lesson with your students until you are confident they are able to do the center independently. Incorporate the recording sheet if appropriate.

Teacher Tip

- This activity takes a lot of practice. It will be difficult for some children to think of questions to ask the reader. You may want to keep a copy of suggested questions at the center for the listener to ask the reader.

Keep in Mind: The primary focus of this communication activity is to generate language between students.

Extension Idea

- Have your students create posters to try and convince their peers to read their book.

Home Connection: Have students discuss a book or article a family member has read. Have student make a list of questions he or she asked the family member and what the responses to those questions were.

Book Talk

Name _____

Author _____

Title _____

I liked this book or story because . . . _____

_____

_____

I gave my book talk to _____

Book Talk

1. Tell your partner the **title** and the **author** of the book you read.

2. Talk about the **beginning**, the **middle**, and the **end** of the book.

3. Talk about the **characters** and **settings**.

4. Answer **questions** about your book.

5. Give **two reasons** why you liked or disliked the story or book.

Optional: Fill out the Book Talk recording sheet.

Convince Me

Objective: Provides independent practice using a graphic organizer or a web to organize a writing piece.

What You Will Need

- Convince Me graphic organizer (page 158)
- Topic Sentence Cards (pages 161–164)
- pencils

Create It

1. Provide the items noted above at the center.
2. Enlarge the graphic organizer or create an overhead to model the activity.

Teach It

Display a copy of the web that is shown on the Convince Me recording sheet. Choose a Topic Sentence Card and write the sentence in the center of the web. Read the sentence out loud and ask your students to help you write reasons to support the topic sentence. Ask students to volunteer reasons that support the topic sentence. Write one reason in each box that branches out from the web.

For example: The topic sentence is "Recess should be longer." Some convincing sentences might be:

- We need exercise.
- Fresh air is good for us.
- I like to see my friends.

Do this lesson with your students until you are confident they are able to do the center independently.

Teacher Tip

- Make certain students have prior knowledge of the topic.

Keep in Mind: Decrease/increase the number of support details required if your students are struggling or finishing too quickly.

Extension Idea

- Have students write the details in paragraph form, including a topic sentence and a concluding sentence.

Home Connection: Have students make a web at home to try to convince their family members of something they would like to do. Don't forget the topic sentence and supporting details.

Convince Me

Reason

_____

- - - - - - - - - - - - - - - -

_____

- - - - - - - - - - - - - - - -

_____

Reason

_____

- - - - - - - - - - - - - - - -

_____

- - - - - - - - - - - - - - - -

_____

Topic Sentence

_____

- - - - - - - - - - - - - - - -

_____

- - - - - - - - - - - - - - - -

_____

Reason

_____

- - - - - - - - - - - - - - - -

_____

Convince Me

The best thing
about school is ___.

Bike riders should
wear helmets.

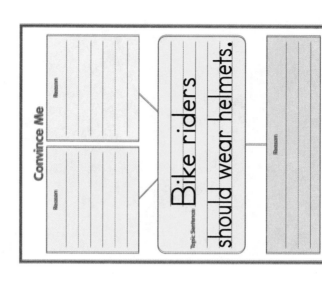

Convince Me

Reason

Reason

Topic Sentence

Bike riders
should wear helmets.

Reason

1. Choose a topic sentence card.

2. Write the topic sentence on the web.

3. Give three reasons to support the topic sentence.

Convince Me

Topic Sentence Cards

Our school is the best school in town.

Tourists should visit my state.

Babies need excercise.

You should read everyday.

My mom makes the best _____ in the world.

Every toddler needs a teddy bear.

Topic Sentence
Cards

Topic Sentence
Cards

Topic Sentence
Cards

Topic Sentence
Cards

Topic Sentence
Cards

Topic Sentence
Cards

162

Convince Me

Topic Sentence Cards

The _____ is the best looking car.

Bike riders should wear helmets.

Recess should be longer.

People should not litter.

_____ _____ is the best television show.

The best thing about school is _____.

Topic Sentence Cards

Topic Sentence Cards

Topic Sentence Cards

Topic Sentence Cards

Topic Sentence Cards

Topic Sentence Cards

Would You Rather?

Objective: Provides independent practice reading, writing, and reasoning.

What You Will Need

- Would You Rather? recording sheet (page 166)
- Would You Rather? cards (pages 169–172)
- pencils

Create It

1. Cut apart the Would You Rather? cards.
2. Provide the items noted above at a center.

Teach It

Students respond to questions. Select one of the Would You Rather? cards. Present the question to the class. Have students volunteer which of the two choices they would rather be or do. Model for your students how to rewrite the question to state their opinion.

Example: I would rather own a dump truck than a unicycle because it can go faster. Be sure students give reasons to support their statement. Demonstrate writing the response on the board.

Do this lesson with your students until you are confident they are able to do the center independently.

Teacher Tip

- Explain to your students that they will need to support each statement with a reason.

Keep in Mind: Some students may want to add pictures to their writing or answers.

Extension Idea

- Have students give supporting facts for their choices.

Home Connection: Have students ask their family members a "Would You Rather?" question. Have students record their responses.

Would You Rather?

Name _____

Card Number

Directions: Rewrite the sentence to state your opinion.

I would rather

because

Would You Rather?

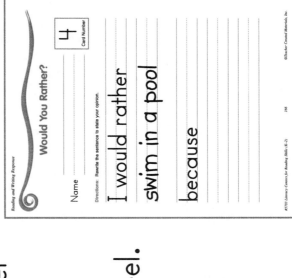

1. Pick a *Would You Rather?* Card and read the card.

2. Write your name and the card number on the recording sheet.

3. Rewrite the sentence. Tell how you feel.

Would You Rather?

Cards

1. Would you rather own a unicycle or a dump truck?

2. Would you rather be able to fly or to walk in space?

3. Would you rather be a goldfish or a guppy?

4. Would you rather swim in a pool or run through a sprinkler?

5. Would you rather swing or ride a bike?

6. Would you rather take a bath or a shower?

Would You Rather?

Sentences   Sentences

Sentences   Sentences

Sentences   Sentences

Would You Rather?

Cards

7. Would you rather eat spaghetti or macaroni and cheese?

8. Would you rather go to work with your mom or your dad?

9. Would you rather learn to fly a rocket or a spaceship?

10. Would you rather be a police officer or a firefighter?

11. Would you rather be a doctor for people or for pets?

12. Would you rather have a brother or a sister?

Sentences   Sentences

Sentences   Sentences

Sentences   Sentences

Retell the Story

Objective: Provides independent practice identifying the elements of a story to retell it.

What You Will Need

- previously read narrative story
- craft sticks (3 or 4 per student)
- crayons or markers
- 4" x 6" (10 cm x 15 cm) index cards (3 or 4 per student)
- stapler or glue
- white copy paper or construction paper
- file folders or science display board
- Elements of a Story poster (page 174)

Create It

1. Provide the items listed above at a center so that children can make stick puppets. Include crayons and markers, index cards and craft sticks. Attach the completed character puppets to the craft sticks with glue or a stapler.
2. Provide paper and crayons or markers to decorate scenery (settings) for the stories.
3. Create a "Little Theater" using file folders or a science display board.
4. Enlarge the Elements of a Story poster. Affix it on or near the theater.

Teach It

Let's review the elements of a story. (Share an enlarged version of the poster.) *There is a plot which has a problem and a solution. There are characters and there is a setting. Today we are going to design some props to help us retell a story. Decide which characters (3 or 4) you will need to reenact the story. Draw each character on an index card. Draw big enough to fill most of the index card's surface. Cut out each character and attach it to a craft stick.*
Next, recreate the setting, or background, of the story. Remember, don't put people or animals in the scene. Place the setting on/in the theater. Now you are ready to retell the story using the character puppets. Be sure to include the problem and solution in the retelling.

Teacher Tip

- Be sure that students are familiar with the story. Encourage them to practice before doing their presentations.

Keep in Mind: Students often have difficulty limiting the number of characters necessary to retell the plot. Specify how many characters can be used to retell each story.

Extension Idea

- Have students write the dialogue among the characters.

Home Connection: Take the characters and the setting home and retell the story to family members.

Elements of a Story

Characters

A story's characters are the people and animals in it.

Setting

A story's setting tells where and when the story takes place.

Plot

Problem

The story's problem is a conflict, disagreement, or trouble concerning one (or more) main character.

Solution

A story's solution is the answer to the problem.

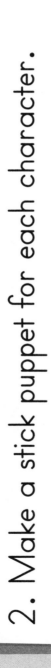

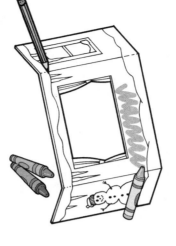

Retell the Story

1. Identify characters from the story.

2. Make a stick puppet for each character.

3. Draw the setting and place it in the theater.

4. Retell the story using the stick puppets.